THE ADVENTURES OF KEHTEAU

Written by Larry Spotted Crow Mann –
Citizen of the Hassanamisco Nipmuc Tribe

Illustrated by Robert Peters Jr. –
Citizen of the Mashpee Wampanoag Tribe

"Kehteau" character modeled after Kehteau A. Mann –
Citizen of the Hassanamisco Nipmuc Tribe

Nipmuc Homelands Map created by Dr. Kim Frasure, Geospatial Arts Maps

CrowStorm™ Publishing 2023

ISBN 9798218306298

THE ADVENTURES OF KEHTEAU

(Native Explorer Series) A curriculum using Indigenous Storytelling to promote Social Development Skills in Early Education throughout the series, for all Tribal Nations and children around the world. The main character is a young Nipmuc boy. *Nipmuc* means, "The People of The Fresh Water" in the Algonquian language. The Nipmuc Tribal homelands are in Central Massachusetts, Northern Connecticut, Northern Rhode Island, and Southern New Hampshire. Kehteau will explore different Tribal Lands across Indian Country. His journey will foster Life Skills such as sharing, communication, empathy, cooperation, and conflict resolution. Additionally, we will learn of the various Tribal traditions, lands, languages and celebrate the strengths found in Indigenous pedagogy. Through Storytelling we learn of Indigenous Peoples' history, survival, and culture.

A Massachusetts Tribal homeland map is included at the end of the book.

The Adventures of Kehteau *is a wonderful story that illustrates the joy of exploring. It shows the importance of helping and making new friends while also teaching vocabulary and culture to young readers. The main character Kehteau teaches about empathy, caring and sharing throughout the story and also highlights the value of family time as he explores with his grandfather. The lessons in this story not only support the understanding of emotions and problem solving, but also depicts bravery, positive social engagement, and the overall joy of learning new things.*

— Brett Random, MSW
Executive Director, Berkshire County Head Start

Hi, I am Kehteau!

"I like to play!"

"I like to explore!"

"I look around!"

"...and I am never bored. There is always something fun to do!"

"Today I will travel from my Nipmuc homelands to the Wampanoag homelands. My Grandfather is taking me for a walk on the beach. We will gather clams and Quahogs to eat."

*The Wampanoag homelands are on the southern coast of Massachusetts, from Weymouth, Cape Cod, and the islands of Nantucket and Martha's Vineyard, and southeast as far as Warren, Rhode Island.

"Then Grandfather will carve the Quahog shells
into beautiful Wampum. Let's go!"

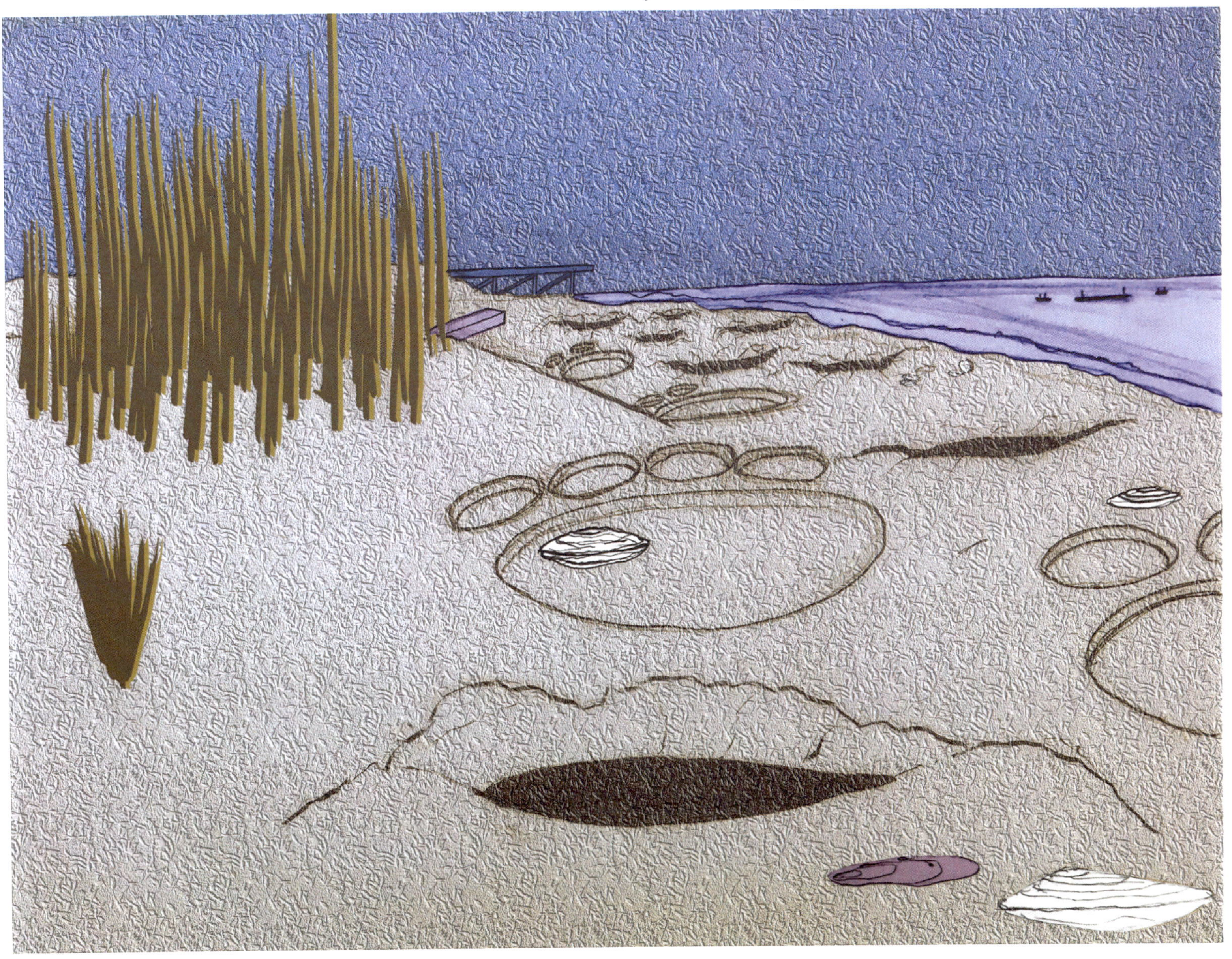

*Quahog – Hard shell clam. The purple and white on the inner shell is what wampum is made from.
*Wampum – Beads carved from Quahog shells. Used to tell stories and seen as a sign of status.

"Oh no, look! There's a Turtle stuck on his back. Let's help him!" "Thank you," said Turtle. "I am Tunuppa. What is your name?"

"I am Kehteau. I like to play. I like to explore. I look around and I'm never bored."

*Tunuppa – Turtle in the Wampanoag language.

"Would you like to come to the beach with Grandfather and I?" asked Kehteau.
"Why yes, I would like that very much!" replied Tunuppa.

"All this walking has made me hungry!" said Kehteau as his stomach growled. "Where can we find something to eat?"

"Look! Weatchimin growing in the dunes!
WOW! I love Weatchimin!"

*Weatchimin – Nipmuc word for corn.

"The stalks are too tall for me to reach. I need help," said Kehteau.
"I can help," said Crow. Kehteau was thankful. "Kuttabotomish Crow," he said.

*Kuttabotomish –"Thank you very much" in the Nipmuc Language.

What is your name?" asked Crow. "I am Kehteau," he answered happily. "I like to play, I like to explore. I look around and I'm never bored." "It's good to meet you Kehteau, I am Konkontoo," replied Crow.

"Would you like to join us for a walk to the beach?" asked Kehteau and Tunuppa. "I would love to join you," replied Konkontoo.

*Konkontoo – Crow in the Nipmuc language.

Grandfather begins to dig in the sand for clams before going to search for Quahogs in the bay.

Kehteau, Tunuppa, and Konkontoo join Grandfather in searching for clams.

They are all having a hard time finding any clams.

Kehteau, Tunuppa, and Konkontoo were getting discouraged.

Grandfather gave up on finding clams and
waded into the low tidewater searching for Quahogs.

Bear, who was nearby, was not having a hard time at all.
He was using his big paws to rake and pull clams out of the sand.

"Oh look," says Kehteau.
"Bear has a whole lot of clams and Quahogs. Let's go visit Bear!"

As they arrived, Bear growled. "Who, are you?" he asked. "Hello Bear, I am Kehteau. I like to play, I like to explore, I look around and I'm never bored. Will you share some clams and Quahogs with us?"

"I am Mosq, and these belong to me and me alone.
I will not share. And I do not care!"

*Mosq – Nipmuc word for bear.

"Why won't you share?" Kehteau asked.
"Because nobody has ever shared anything with me," Mosq replied.

"Today I will share with you, Mosq," Kehteau said cheerfully. "Take some of my Weatchimin. Konkontoo the Crow shared with me, now I will share with you."

"And Kehteau helped me when I was stuck on my back,"
said Tunuppa. "We all helped each other."

"Yes," said Mosq. "Yes. Sharing is nice after all. Thank you for the Weatchimin. This makes me happy. I will share some Quahogs."

"Kuttabotomish, Mosq!" said Kehteau.

Grandfather was happy that Mosq shared. So he carved necklaces for Mosq, Konkontoo, Tunuppa, and Kehteau out of the Quahog shells.

Grandfather gathered them all in a circle and explained the meaning of his gifts. "When we share and help each other, we bring joy and love to our family and friends."

The End

CAN YOU POINT TO WHERE KEHTEAU IS FROM?

SUGGESTED QUESTIONS FOR STUDENTS

1. Who is the main character(s)?
   Is there one word that comes to mind when you think about this character?
   How is he/she like you?

2. Where does the story take place?
   Is it a real place?

3. Does anything in this book seem familiar to you?

4. Who is your favorite character?
   What do you like about them?
   Do you remember the characters names?
   Do you remember what their names mean?

5. Can you think of a time you shared with someone?
   How did it make you feel?
   How do you think it made them feel?

6. Do you remember what helped Mosq want to share?

7. How do the people in the story use Quahog shells?

8. Did you learn anything new from reading this book?
   Tell me something you learned?
   Who will you tell about what you learned?

GLOSSARY

Kehteau (pronounced - Key- Tay- O) is the Nipmuc word for "he who has been here since the beginning."

Quahog (pronounced Co-Hog) is a hard white and purple clam that is native to the eastern shores of North America and Central America.

Many tribes carve the shells into beads called Wampum. The beads are made into all types of jewelry and wampum belts which become a sacred part of their culture, spirituality, and stories.

Weatchimin (pronounced Wheat-Cha-Min) is the Nipmuc word for corn. Did you know that Native Americans created corn into what it is today?

Mosq (pronounced Mosk) is the Nipmuc word for Bear.

Kuttabotomish (pronounced Kutta-Ba-Toh-Mish) means "thank you very much" in the Nipmuc language.

Tunuppa (pronounced Ton-Nuppa) – Turtle in Wampanoag language.

Konkontoo (pronounced Con-Con-Two) – Crow in the Nipmuc language.

To Learn more about the Nipmuc Tribe visit **www.nipmucband.org**

To Learn more about the Wampanoag tribe visit **mashpeewampanoagtribe-nsn.gov**

To learn about the Ohketeau Cultural Center visit **www.ohketeau.org**

ACKNOWLEDGMENTS

As a dear friend once reminded me: (Thanks Carlos) we humans are pack animals. Making connections, supporting, caring, uplifting, and sharing our experiences together is how we have managed to thrive as a species. So here is to my Pack who have brought their own special skill, insight, artistic development, scholarship, and love to this book.

First off, my partner, my best friend, my love, Riena Antunez. She was instrumental in the initial stages of concept curriculum development and continues to be part of the supporting process.

To one of my best friends ever, Brian Chenevert who shared his talents, insight, and support during the beginning stages of development.

Robert Peters Sr., we have been lifelong friends and grown up and "older" together as we watched the ever-changing tides of our communities. Kuttabotomish, to you, for taking the time to work on the illustrations and visionary development of this process.

To Robert Peters Jr., thank you for taking my words and creating the beautiful images and scenes that made the story a multi adventurous experience. You have far exceeded my expectations!

Dr. Kim Frashure, thank you for creating an original Nipmuc homelands map using scientific methods of hydrology, historical documents, and geospatial analysis. I can't thank you enough for your friendship, support, and ongoing collaboration on numerous projects. This has certainly been an amazing one.

Thank you to my good friend and colleague Kevin Wery for supporting this book since its inception.

To Brett Random, thank you for taking the time to review the book and offer your expert and parental support for this series. I appreciate your friendship and loved your wedding!

Karen Greenberg, thank you! After an arduous search to find the right person to help with the set up and design, it was serendipitous to find you. I was impressed with your credentials, expertise and super appreciative of your immediate enthusiasm to take this project on.

To my dear little boy Kehteau, this book is a tribute to you, your ancestors, and all the beauty the future brings for our People.

To all my children, family, friends, Tribal community, Ohketeau Cultural Center, and Double Edge Theatre staff, thank you for the never-ending support and love.

May this book share the spirit of The People of Fresh Water.

Aquene!
— Larry Spotted Crow Mann

ABOUT THE AUTHOR

Larry Spotted Crow Mann is an award-winning writer, poet, cultural educator, Traditional Storyteller, tribal drummer/dancer and motivational speaker involving youth sobriety, cultural and environmental awareness.

He has served his Tribal community for over 30 years and is a founder and Co-Director of the Ohketeau Cultural Center. www.ohketeau.org

He is an enrolled citizen of the Hassanamisco Nipmuc Tribe of Massachusetts.

His writings include *Coming Home: Preventing Alcohol and Drug Use Among Native American Teens, A Circle Tied to Mother Earth: Native Life Skills for Middle School Children,* and *Stories and Poems for Northeastern Native Tribal Families.* (All booklets are available through the Massachusetts Health Promotion Clearinghouse.)

His books include *Tales from the Whispering Basket, The Mourning Road to Thanksgiving* and *Drumming & Dreaming.*

He has served as a board member of the Nipmuk Cultural Preservation, which is an organization set up to promote the cultural, social and spiritual needs of Nipmuc people as well as an educational resource of Native American studies.

Mann also serves as a Review Committee Member, at The Native American Poets Project at the Peabody Museum of Archaeology & Ethnology.

Mann is also the first Native American to sing the opening Honor Song and Land Acknowledgement at the 2021 Boston Marathon Starting Line, and the recipient of the 2021 Indigenous Peoples Award of the Berkshire County Branch of the NAACP.

whisperingbasket.com

www.ingramcontent.com/pod-product-compliance
Ingram Content Group UK Ltd.
Pitfield, Milton Keynes, MK11 3LW, UK
UKRC032322290726
14090UKWH00005B/413

* 9 7 9 8 2 1 8 3 0 6 2 9 8 *